MINERS
Cocoanut Oil
SHAMPOO

A perfect Cleanser
for Hair and Scalp

After using, dry hair,
apply EVAROSA HAIR
TONIC to keep scalp

Nora Murphy's
Country House Style

MAKING YOUR HOME A COUNTRY HOUSE

Nora Murphy's
Country House Style

MAKING YOUR HOME A COUNTRY HOUSE

Nora Murphy

with Deborah Golden

Photography by DuAnne Simon

VENDOME

NEW YORK · LONDON

CONTENTS

The Elements of Country House Style

I was seven years old when I stepped into the small, white Cape Cod–style house that changed my life. It was a gem, perfectly tucked behind a gracious Colonial mansion in Southport, Connecticut, just a stone's throw away from the beach on Long Island Sound. The little house—and the big one—belonged to Mrs. Gilman, a kind and artistic woman whose primary residence was in Manhattan, on Sutton Place. Before we knew her, the mansion was the only house on the property. But one year, as a birthday gift, her husband had the little Cape built as a studio for her creative endeavors.

Mama would help Mrs. G. at her cocktail and dinner parties, and I, a very shy little girl, would tag along from time to time. Her place was only a few miles from our 1920s house, a handyman special in Fairfield, but oh, it was a world away. (Our house was in rough shape when we got it, but my parents were up to the challenge. They did all the repairs themselves, so I saw firsthand how a home could be

left Is there any better way to say "welcome"? Armfuls of branches from my ancient rhododendron greet visitors to my Connecticut country house.

transformed with the right ideas and some hard work. Those lessons survive in me, and in my husband, Rick, today. Minus a few specialties, like hanging plaster, we continue to tackle just about every project that needs doing.)

Mama and I loved Mrs. G.'s spirit, and I loved everything in and about her studio. It was warm and inviting. Cozy, but airy and bright. It felt happy—livable and comfortable. She decorated with antiques, which I wouldn't know much about for years, but I knew that every piece had a story and that it was chosen with love. The place got into my soul. (That's a big statement, but I think I can back it up: My dining room is furnished with an old pine harvest table surrounded by Windsor chairs. Glancing at them one day a few years ago, Mama commented that they were "just like Mrs. G.'s." Coincidence? It sure doesn't feel like one!) Hers was my first true country house: not so much a place as a state of mind—warm, welcoming, and deeply beautiful.

That house sparked a fire in me: a passion for interior design, classic style, and great new ideas. A passion for spaces that, no matter where they are, feel like her studio did—like all the homes in this book do. A country house doesn't look any one way. It might be in a suburban neighborhood in the Midwest, or in a former tavern deep in New England, or in a prefab home on a postage-stamp lot in a city. But all of them are friendly and warm. They all have caretakers, like me, who share a love of history and a deep devotion to the idea that every little thing they do creates a much bigger picture. (I think of us as caretakers because these homes had lives before they knew us, and will continue to after we're gone—and because you don't have to own a home to live a country house life.) We all have an open-door policy—outside is in, inside is out, everyone is welcome. We have no time for the precious—everything is usable, in its way—yes, even (especially!) the antiques. We share a passion.

Imagine an atmosphere of warmth and welcome, both down to earth and elegant. It rolls with the rhythm of the seasons. It has an easy grace, and it's surprisingly simple to switch on. It makes you feel happy and creative, content and refreshed, surrounded by beauty, loved, and most important, at home—no matter where you live. That's country house style. That's the feeling I wish for you.

opposite Handmade meets nature-made is a classic country house style combination. Scallops and curves play together, turning this unlikely duo—a hand-painted sign that once marked the boundary of a nearby town and half of a giant clamshell—into a simple, fresh, sculptural moment.

My approach is simple. It's about styling more than "being a designer"; about rules of thumb rather than orders of operation; about snippets of info, not volumes; and always, *always* about real life. It's so easy to live this way, wherever you call home. It's not a point on a map. Country house style thrives a moment at a time. It's a little romantic, a little nostalgic, and all about a simplicity that everyone can share. Let me show you how.

But first, let's chat about the why. I've long loved the idea of a "year-round retreat"—treating the place I live in like a lovely escape from the everyday. A second home on a one-home budget. The birth of country house style!

From my childhood home to my college dorm rooms to my first apartment and then my first house, I've approached each place with the same nesting instinct—to make it beautiful *and* warm and comfy.

In each of these places, doing that meant checking the following five boxes. (Does it sound like I'm making rules, after I've just said that's not what this is about? Don't fret. They're not rules! They're the elements that bring that beautiful, warm, comfy home to life.)

- The feeling that the door is always open and you're among friends, exactly where you're supposed to be—it's a place where you are always welcome.
- An old work table in a modern dining room; an antique wood chandelier painted an unexpected color—it's a place where we honor tradition by changing it up.
- There's no room for fussy, but there's definitely room for cozying up and settling in with everything you need close at hand—it's a place where comfort is always in style.
- Having the things you love around you (an item or a collection or three!) is a way to put your heart into where you live—it's a place where there's always room for your favorite things.
- Outside is in. Inside, if it can be, is out. Whether a yard with a garden or a windowsill with a few herbs catching the sun, there's a connection with nature—it's a place where home extends well beyond our walls.

opposite My dining room is my entertaining go-to space; making all who gather here feel loved is the real reason I pour my heart into the details.

So check those boxes. Take that extra minute to make a thoughtful choice about how you set a table, choose a fabric, or decide which flowers to plant, and see what a difference it can make—not just in the outcome, but in how it makes you feel!

You Are Always Welcome

Warmth. It's the quality that every home with country house style has in common—the feeling that the door is always open and that you're among friends. That you're exactly where you're supposed to be. When you're there, relaxed and comfortable, you know it. I always notice when a home has it—how can you not! It's what I want for everyone who comes to my home.

It resonates through a home that's in tune with the seasons, from the walkway to the door to the entryway, to the sights, sounds, and scents that greet you inside—the layers of thoughtfulness that create a wonderful welcome. When a bowl of freshly popped popcorn awaits by the fireplace. When soft music is playing as you walk through the door. When you're always greeted with happiness and a big hug.

It's the way a simple tomato salad from the kitchen garden becomes a feast—you can feel the love of growing it, making it, styling it, serving it, enjoying it, and everything else before, after, and in between. It's two chairs and a table set under a shade tree, and a pitcher of fresh, cold lemonade. It's a cheerful bucket of just-cut flowers from the garden. It's a spot near the door where you can sit to pull off (or put on) your boots.

It's all in the details, how the little things add up to something big and wonderful—how we make each other feel special, appreciated, welcome—one small moment at a time.

We Honor Tradition by Changing It Up

Country house style wouldn't be possible without a love of tradition. We respect what came before, we gather its stories to share, we seek out the beauty in some element of the simplicity of the past. Oh, simplicity—maybe the strongest link in the chain that connects us all.

opposite A mantelpiece in the 1767 part of our home holds many memories of our favorite vacations at the shore. The gilded fish was once perched atop an old Cape Cod home; in the nineteenth-century oval frame is a portrait by Nantucket artist Kolene Spicher.

It's bringing tradition into today that keeps it fresh and exciting. It's appreciating the beauty of antiques, imperfect and timeworn, in a hands-on way. It's living *with* tradition, but not inside it, mixing the best of old and new, hard and soft, textural and smooth. It's embracing the classics and breaking (some of!) the rules.

It's finding balance, like adding antiques to a modern space, or the unexpected placement of something new in a room defined by time-honored treasures: using beautiful antique textiles for everyday living; setting a formal table with crumpled linen napkins and an unconventional centerpiece; grounding a room of family heirlooms with a low-maintenance sisal rug.

It's the element of surprise, like exposing the frame of a masterfully built antique chair, without reupholstering it.

It mixes styles and materials, welcomes historical bits and pieces, and gives you the freedom to turn "any old thing" into a work of art—provided you're willing to have fun with it!

Comfort Is Always in Style

There's no room for fussy here. Country house style is simple, honest, and livable.

It's experienced through all the senses. These are spaces for cozying up and settling in: sofas that invite you to put up your feet; deep wing chairs made for curling up in for contemplation or conversation. Layers of softness—a plush pillow here, a chunky throw there, texture wherever possible.

Candles flicker warmly; a fire in the hearth crackles and draws you close. Something simple and delicious is on the stove, in the oven, or in your hands. Scents set a mood—lilacs, firewood, simmering stews, fresh tomatoes, baking bread—whatever you find comforting is what should surround you. Like scent, a little music helps remind you to breathe in deeply and exhale your tensions away. All the conveniences close at hand make living here feel natural and easy—and visiting here feel like a B & B where any need is satisfied before you even have to ask.

It's the soothing retreat from the world outside, a haven and a respite where you re-center and recharge. However you put it together, the result is

opposite Comfortable wing chairs with easy-care slipcovers flank an old tea table in front of the library wall we designed in our bedroom. It's a cozy space for curling up with a good book.

the simple joy of contentment: life with a place for everything, and everything in its place.

There's Always Room for Our Favorite Things

I'm a collector by nature. Part of me loves the thrill of the hunt. Part of me can't get enough of the stories that come with so many of my favorite things. But all of me knows that making sure there's a place for what you love, so that you can see and enjoy it every day, is key to country house style.

An item or a collection (or two or three) that is meaningful to you gives your home personality—a warmth and a connection that's uniquely yours. Even if you love what someone else loves, you'll probably live with it in your own way. That's part of what makes it beautiful. Special objects are more than the things they are—they're the keepers of sweet memories, the stirrers of emotion.

A walk through a country house is a tour of stories—ask about a French basket and hear the story of a first-anniversary gift, or a bucket of shells, each one brought home from vacation by the children, now grown. How you display, live with, and use your treasures becomes part of their story and yours as well.

Show them in unexpected ways. Move them to different rooms. Rearrange them. They'll feel like new finds again. Create a big impact by displaying an entire collection together, or derive subtle joy from carefully placing your favorite things here and there so you come across them throughout the day.

You don't have to know a thing about antiques to be a collector. You don't have to haunt auction houses or break the bank. If you pick up as many seashells as we do, you don't have to spend any money at all! It's about style and the things that nourish your heart, soul, and, of course, your senses.

Home Extends Well Beyond Our Walls

Country house style blurs the lines between indoors and out. The exterior is just as important to country house living as the interior.

opposite These are a few of our favorite things. Rick, Conor, and I continue to add treasures collected on hikes in the woods, walks on the shore, and visits to our favorite shops and flea markets to this eighteenth-century cupboard—our very own cabinet of curiosities!

One way I expand the indoors out is by building "rooms" outside, whether on my stone patios or around the fire pit by the old rock wall in the back. A thoughtfully planted walk to the front door (or the back) makes a wonderful, welcoming first impression. Consider scale, color, and, of course, scent.

Creating beautiful surroundings for these outdoor spaces is what makes gardening so gratifying. As is the utter peace and joy that comes from spending a day in the dirt. Working with nature is one of life's great pleasures—planting, nurturing, and watching your efforts thrive!

My plantings range from rose beds to mixed perennials to thick daylily borders, all anchored by mature shrubs like rhododendron and weigela. My white picket-fenced kitchen garden is a room all its own. The foundation is there, and I move things around each year to change it up . . . just as I do inside!

Country house style is about the endless pursuit of finding new ways to lure the outdoors in. I like to pot plants and perennials from the nursery to enjoy them inside, and then plant them in the garden when it's time to refresh. From big bouquets of forsythia and mock orange branches to smaller bunches of daffodils and daisies, anything that blooms can bring beauty and joy.

The people you'll meet in this book live in all kinds of homes—old and new; in towns, suburbs, cities, and out in the country. Their styles, like their personalities, are delightfully diverse—no two alike, and all different from mine.

Wendy's evokes Swedish style, artful and austere in the most wonderful way. Dana's is all Americana, rustic and modern at the same time. Amy's has the heart of a sweet château: pretty, pastel, and romantic. Tessa's is preppy, traditional, and charming, so like an English cottage. And Shawn and Kris's has an outdoorsy, upscale cabin vibe.

Each home, though, is cared for kindly and thoughtfully. Nothing's precious, everything's used and well loved, and the details matter. The most important thing they have in common with one another, with my home—and with yours!—is that they're all warm and welcoming places where real people lead their normal lives. They're all perfect expressions of the many ways there are to live with country house style.

opposite As soon as the weather allows, we start living outside again. Anywhere there's space for a chair or two and a table, you can create an outdoor room.

Some words—*story, caretaker, sharing, warm*—are mentioned a lot throughout the book. Everyone who participated in it used them. But I've come to realize that they stand for so much more. They're the common threads of our entire community, and that is what we are: a community of friends who may not have met yet, but whose love for this *feeling* of home defines how we live and how we want to live. As we sifted through the thousands of photographs we took for this book, I was tickled to see other common threads emerge. We discovered that everyone has flowers at the front door, open shelves in the kitchen, and some kind of kitchen island. Shawn and Amy each came up with innovative uses for transferware. Wendy and Tessa are queens of textiles. Dana and Shawn have barns that serve as their studios. Tessa, Dana, and I have a bit of a shell fixation. Yet our individual treatments of country house style are all different.

I'm grateful every day for my Connecticut Country House blog, and all the connections it's made—between you and me, and among you, too. It's how most of the people in this book and I found each other, in a series of seemingly unconnected events. Some of the people you'll meet here I've been lucky enough to call my friends for years. Others came into my life through the blog, and this book has been a wonderful reason to finally connect face to face.

And now *you're* here. All I can say is, I've been very, very lucky. All the way back to that first day when Mrs. G. welcomed me into the little Cape that changed everything.

opposite Stepping into a country house is like entering the hearts of the people who live there. Everything in this entry represents something dear to us—my love of gardening, Rick's love of fishing, Conor's love of hiking in the woods—and it can change with the seasons or the occasion.

MY COUNTRY HOUSE

I loved my home well before we officially "met." For ten years I drove past it at least once a week on the way to my parents' house in southern Connecticut. Every single time I drove by, I would slow down, crane my neck as far as I dared to get another good look, and think, "Boy, the people who live there are so lucky!"

I can't quite put my finger on why I was so smitten with the place. Could it have been its location, set back on a picture-perfect country road with no neighboring houses in sight? Could it have been the way it was nestled in the hollow of rocky cliffs and woods? Could it have been the simple historical provenance of the little saltbox? Whatever it was, it surely had my attention.

When the "For Sale" sign went up, I couldn't make the call fast enough.

The Realtor ushered us in through the back, and in a single glance at the handcrafted eighteenth-century details I knew that the interior matched—no, exceeded—all my expectations. I was almost disappointed that it was as wonderful as it was. After all, we had a lovely home in the same town, a home I'd showered with care and attention. We weren't even looking! But I looked. And that was it.

Everything about the house was so simple, yet so elegant. It's not uncommon for eighteenth-century houses to be dark inside, so I was struck by the light flooding in

left **A point of view.** Each of my gardens offers a different view of my beloved home, and I can see a garden from every room in the house. There's a strong connection between inside and out in country house style.

through windows set with 9-over-6 panes of wavy antique glass. The sun bathed the plaster walls and ceilings, revealing their little bows and ripples in the warm, natural light. The original pine floor was slanted downward, and when I turned on the cellar lights, I could see the light coming up through the wider gaps in the flooring. It was *fabulous*.

The pièce de résistance of the living room was an amazing cooking fireplace that took up most of the main wall. The gourmet kitchen (an upgrade by the most recent owner) boasted a cathedral ceiling, nineteenth-century beams (original to the barn on the property), and antique wood cabinetry, crafted from the floorboards of the barn. I could see myself prepping and cooking at the overscale island and industrial stove. The dining room's huge picture windows framed breathtaking views of the gardens, stone walls, and woods. On the second floor I found three simple, almost primitive bedrooms—two tiny, and the third . . . let's just say less tiny.

This was the house I had been dreaming of since I was a little girl wishing that Mrs. G.'s Cape were my own. (And, like Mrs. Gilman's, this really had been the "country house" of a New York couple in the mid-1900s. It did indeed have the atmosphere of a time that seemed more joyful and relaxed—full circle!) Never did I really believe I would live in such a special place. I fell hard for this incredible 1767 Connecticut country house, which I share with my husband, Rick ("Murph"); our son, Conor; and our pup, Fiona. It's my muse. This is where and why the Nora Murphy Connecticut Country House blog was born. It's here that I write, cook, garden, shoot thousands of photographs, write, tape TV shows, write, entertain, share my love of simple, down-to-earth pleasures that we all can enjoy, and above all, live.

right **Incorporate natural elements.** My country house is home to ever-changing arrangements of natural things. Clamshells from Nantucket, heart-shaped beach rocks in a glass bowl, and a mossy concrete planter packed with geraniums mix indoors with out and old with new.

above, clockwise from top **All that sparkles.** New, creamy-white mats freshen up a set of eighteenth-century engravings from London in mismatched frames; Ethan Allen's modern take on an eighteenth-century sconce glitters with more than 200 hand-set mirrors; a seeded-glass jar holds ephemera of daily life: old photos, ticket stubs, handwritten notes, childhood art.

preceding pages **Make an entrance.** Songbirds chirp all around our house, so this entry hall seemed an ideal spot for a flock of eighteenth-century François-Nicolas Martinet engravings. To create an easy and inexpensive gallery wall, dress new frames in a coat of milk paint, as I did here.

opposite **Be bold.** A black stepback cupboard houses our TV and plenty more. Country house style always has room for modern touches.

above, clockwise from top left **All this useful beauty.** Old watering cans are utilitarian works of art—the feel of the handles, the interesting shapes of the spouts; a large English basket I use for weeding in the garden also makes a statement as a centerpiece; a grouping of antique boxes and baskets adds texture, style, and useful storage.

pages 32–33 and preceding pages **Everything old is new again.** A fresh coat of white paint throughout the house draws attention to all that's well loved and beautifully worn while keeping each space feeling modern and clean.

opposite **Pot up perennials.** An iron tuteur gives shape to plumes of catmint in an old Swedish herring bucket. I love that balance of sculptural and untamed! Keep a lookout—tuteurs are easy flea market finds.

opposite **Back to basics.** Country house style means making something special with what you've got. Most of my table settings start with two things: glasses from my collection of La Rochere and white dinnerware from Home Goods. You don't need a fancy foundation to create a flight of fancy.

preceding pages **Not-so-secret indoor garden.** An eighteenth-century European mural on a wood panel floats behind large copper trays of azalea topiaries—a garden scene that keeps me thinking spring on even the grayest winter day.

above **Quick-change artistry.** Changing the linen and flatware, adding chargers and placemats, and swapping fauna for flora give the same table a very different look.

opposite **Pantry styling 101.** A very old, barn-red Pennsylvania pantry holds everyday dishes. Open shelving is convenient, lets collections be seen, and encourages the warm, reach-in-and-help-yourself conviviality of country house style.

above **Form takes the cake.** A chunk of staghorn coral turns a cake stand into art.

above, clockwise from top left **Keeping in rhythm with the seasons.** Apples, so plentiful in the fall, will stay fresh for a week or two on the counter; berries are the gift that keeps on giving: they're hardy, they proliferate, and the right assortment in your garden means you can harvest spring through fall; tying on an apron always makes me feel ready to get to work.

preceding pages **Welcome to the hub.** Upcycling is a staple of country house style, and so are creative solutions. The kitchen island's top was made of reclaimed floorboards from the more than century-old barn out back. The checkerboard-patterned painted floor lends rustic charm to what lies beneath—planks of 1970s yellow oak.

opposite **Kid stuff.** Children's art adds an instant dose of whimsy, color, happiness, and, once that child is older, sweet memories.

opposite **It had to have a story.** We knew from day one that the tiny, low-ceilinged bedrooms upstairs meant that we'd have to make some changes, but building a new addition didn't feel like the answer. What did? A dilapidated chicken coop that crossed my path online one day. The 1857 structure was a mess, but I saw beautiful possibilities in its elegant bones, huge windows, and charming cupola. Moving the Coop from Massachusetts and renovating it was one of the most satisfying projects I've ever taken on.

above **My love of Americana.** All the furnishings in the Coop have a modern country/Americana vibe. The elegance of the original building is still evident in its high, vaulted ceiling, exposed posts and beams, and plank walls.

opposite **Balance in all things.** In its summer finery, the bed is dressed in white and peony-pink cotton and linen with a ruffle here and there and botanical embroidery on the top sheet and shams. I designed the library wall to look like shelving in an old general store—big, sturdy, and utilitarian—so introducing that bit of "pretty" was key to soften the space.

above **Tea (table) for two.** The first owner of this tea table took it home more than 250 years ago; I use it every day and love being the custodian of another chapter in its long story.

opposite **Think outside the box.** Before we renovated the Coop, the fence seen in the mirror was part of a wall; now it's our shower enclosure. (We couldn't resist the idea of an outdoor shower indoors!) The mirror is another repurposed piece: a double-hung window from New York's Flatiron Building fitted with mirror glass by an antiques dealer.

above **Make it user-friendly.** An old wooden plate rack, hung upside down and painted the same color as the walls, makes a perfect towel rack. The reproduction faucet is unvarnished; it will develop a rich, authentic patina over time.

opposite **Dig in the dirt.** Lettuces love cooler temperatures and a little bit of shade, so they're early occupants of the kitchen garden each spring.

above, clockwise from top left **Kitchen and cutting gardens.** The kitchen garden, with its neat rows of herbs, veggies, and berries, was a dream that's recently come true; coneflowers are the summer feature in the miniature boxwood–bordered perennial gardens out front; annuals like cosmos thrive in big clay pots all summer.

preceding pages **Heaven scent.** These lusciously fragrant Eden roses grow on bushes that are older than Conor; abundant Fairy spray roses bloom alongside them each June.

above **A reimagined master bedroom suite.** The Coop in all its glory. The integrity of its nineteenth-century architecture connects seamlessly with the eighteenth-century house. Its brick foundation, front door, wall of windows (minus some panes), and grand cupola are all original. It reshaped not only the way we live inside but also the configuration of the property's gardens and walkways.

overleaf **Anatomy of a country house.** From the far left: the Coop; the original 1767 saltbox, which includes the living room and summer room, and three tiny bedrooms and a bath upstairs; the TV nook; the kitchen; and the dining room.

opposite **Grow what you love.** Near the rock wall below the Coop, Lady Alexandra Duff peonies perfume the air for a few glorious weeks each May.

A COUNTRY
HOUSE IN THE
MOUNTAINS

Wendy has been a fixture at Brimfield (New England's largest antiques show and a mecca for anyone on "the hunt") for years. Her tent, the Textile Trunk, is always one of my must-stops—it's almost impossible not to drool over her gorgeous collection of antique European textiles, which range from the eighteenth to the very early twentieth century. In 2016, ever on the lookout for beautiful things to share on my blog, I introduced myself and asked to photograph her exquisite textile vignettes. We've been fast friends ever since.

Wendy's interest in antique textiles began when she and her young family were living in London, and trips to France were easy and frequent. On one of those trips, she came across a piece of eighteenth-century fabric and, in her words, "the heavens opened." Already passionate about history, genealogy, art, and design, Wendy felt a new pull. She began collecting textiles with abandon and even taught herself to sew so that she could give new life to them. Eventually, she realized that she couldn't buy more until she had sold some of what she had. But to become an educated seller of these fabrics, she had to become an authority, and she spent countless hours at the Victoria and Albert Museum in London and at textile museums in France. As her knowledge grew, so did her devotion.

left **A Vermont state of mind.** The Adirondack Mountains of New York, seen from Wendy's backyard. The front of the house faces Vermont's Green Mountains.

Her pared-back style lets the bones of her old house shine. Every sightline is simple and beautiful. Her most treasured discoveries are featured throughout, and everything she chooses to keep—from the pots in the kitchen to a found finial to the fabrics she lives with so effortlessly—feels special. Here, even the functional is art.

It wasn't always so! The first time she saw the 1800 Federal-style house that she shares with her teenage son, Ethan, and daughter, Innogen, the rooms were swathed in wallpaper, the walls and floors were dark, and the room that's now her lovely, light-filled kitchen was a deep hunter green. "Not a single person at the time said, 'This is right for you.' But I knew I could take it to the place I wanted. I knew it was going to be a lot of work, but I wasn't afraid of it."

Her goal was to turn chaos into calm, and she accomplished it beautifully. "I try to be present. Being surrounded by serenity helps that happen. It's also very, very important to me that pieces have a history. I have to know they've been loved and used in the past."

Wendy finds creative ways to keep a selection of textiles in sight. "Just as someone might paint a wall to change a room, I swap textiles. This is my moving gallery, my ever-changing art show." To be sure, at Wendy's country house in the mountains, there's always room for her favorite things.

"I think country house style means comfort and history. It's an aesthetic that makes one feel relaxed, at home, comfortable. I also see it as a reflection of history—how what was utilitarian and inexpensive in the past, like a basket, still has life and purpose." —Wendy

right **Warm and welcoming.** A handcrafted table of reclaimed Vermont barn wood was made especially for the sunny kitchen.

opposite **A refined farmhouse.** Wendy's country house was built about 1800 by a gentleman named Francis Breakenridge. He and his brother built homes in town around the same time, and both are still happily occupied.

overleaf **Architectural sightlines.** Country house style embraces a roll-up-your-sleeves way of life! Wendy stripped and painted the floors herself in the upstairs foyer—one of her favorite spaces in the house. Breakenridge installed the east-facing Palladian window, which has a sweeping view of the Green Mountains and admits incredible natural light.

above **Chalky whites.** Still-life groupings of sculptural architectural fragments pop up all over the house. Wendy looks for "that wonderful chalky tone" before she'll add a piece to the collection. A common finish gives a collection depth.

opposite **Madame et
monsieur.** A French
painted-canvas panel
from the late 1800s once
decorated a château door.

above **Hang a salvaged door.** A friend of Wendy's insisted that he had found the ideal door for her new
kitchen. It was dirty, dusty, and all the glass was painted orange. What vision! Scraped and cleaned, it was
a perfect fit.

opposite **Wide-open spaces.** Like most of my favorite country kitchens, Wendy's has that friendly, reach-in-and-help-yourself vibe.

above, clockwise from left **Flowers, fabrics, and finds.** Mature hydrangeas thrive in the yard; dried hydrangeas and a fragment create another still life near the back door; woven hemp hand towels from Europe have "that wonderful nubby texture I love so much."

preceding pages **Transforming a library.** The open shelves are holdovers from the kitchen's former use as a library. Wendy stripped the floors, painted the walls, and added the sink and the island. The crown molding, from a Vermont salvage shop, is one of her favorite architectural finds.

above **Look for form and function.** Farm-fresh eggs rest in an antique stoneware cheese mold, which once held cheese as the whey drained off. In true country house style, these useful old things have modern forms and serve new functions.

opposite **Add distinctive storage pieces.** As in all our country houses, Wendy's works hard for everyone who lives there. Lunch bags, sunscreen, and sports bottles are stored in an antique cupboard in the kitchen, out of sight but never out of mind.

above, clockwise from top left **Garden inspired.** A nineteenth-century finial rests atop scrims that were backdrops in a nineteenth-century French theater; a remnant of hand-painted Chinese wallpaper, ca. 1740, is a treasured gift; a grouping of French and English quilts, all dating to the eighteenth- and nineteenth-centuries.

preceding pages **How to make an entrance.** In the foyer, a weathered flea market dresser holds another sweet vignette on top and winter gear inside. Nineteenth-century columns, originally meant for a stage Wendy wanted to build in the living room for her children's plays, now flank the entrance to the living room.

opposite **A relaxed style.** The chaise is draped with volumes of hand-woven linen stitched together in the eighteenth century to make a cover for a cart or a wagon.

above **Look for the unusual.** A favorite of Wendy's—and of mine—is a butterfly-shaped antique hatbox she found at Brimfield, our favorite stomping grounds for antiques, and where we met. Although it's a bit more colorful, it has the same chalky tone she loves in her architectural fragments.

opposite **Create a vignette.** When French shepherds took their flocks to the field for the day, they also took an umbrella for shelter from the sun. Wendy has found a few in her travels.

Captain G. A. Beale-Browne.

above, clockwise from left **The beauty of antique textiles.** Hemp grain sacks were hard-working everyday objects in eighteenth- and nineteenth-century Europe; the trim is from the 1700s, part of a French hand-woven ikat fabric called Flamme that was mostly used in bedding; lace from a skirt that was made for *une mademoiselle* about 1900.

opposite **Invest in the best.** Though Wendy sells many of her textiles, these are part of her personal collection. Most are from the 1700s, and each is a work of art.

above **Feel the quality.** A peek into Wendy's bedroom reveals the duvet cover she made of antique French linen sheets. Though only two and a half sheets were used, the cover weighs nearly ten pounds!

overleaf **Finding peace and tranquillity.** Wendy's favorite thing about her home is . . .? "The windows. All day, every day, end of story. Some of the panes are original, and the wavy glass casts patterns. It's like there's always a new piece of art, depending on the light. I get deeply happy when I see it dance and sparkle." Her salvaged tub faces the west-facing arched window, with its gorgeous view of the sunset over the mountains. Heaven!

opposite **Worn in a storied past.** If you've ever wondered what French mussels fishermen wore to work a hundred years ago, now you know! The boots are charmingly tucked into a pretty cupboard from (where else?!) Brimfield.

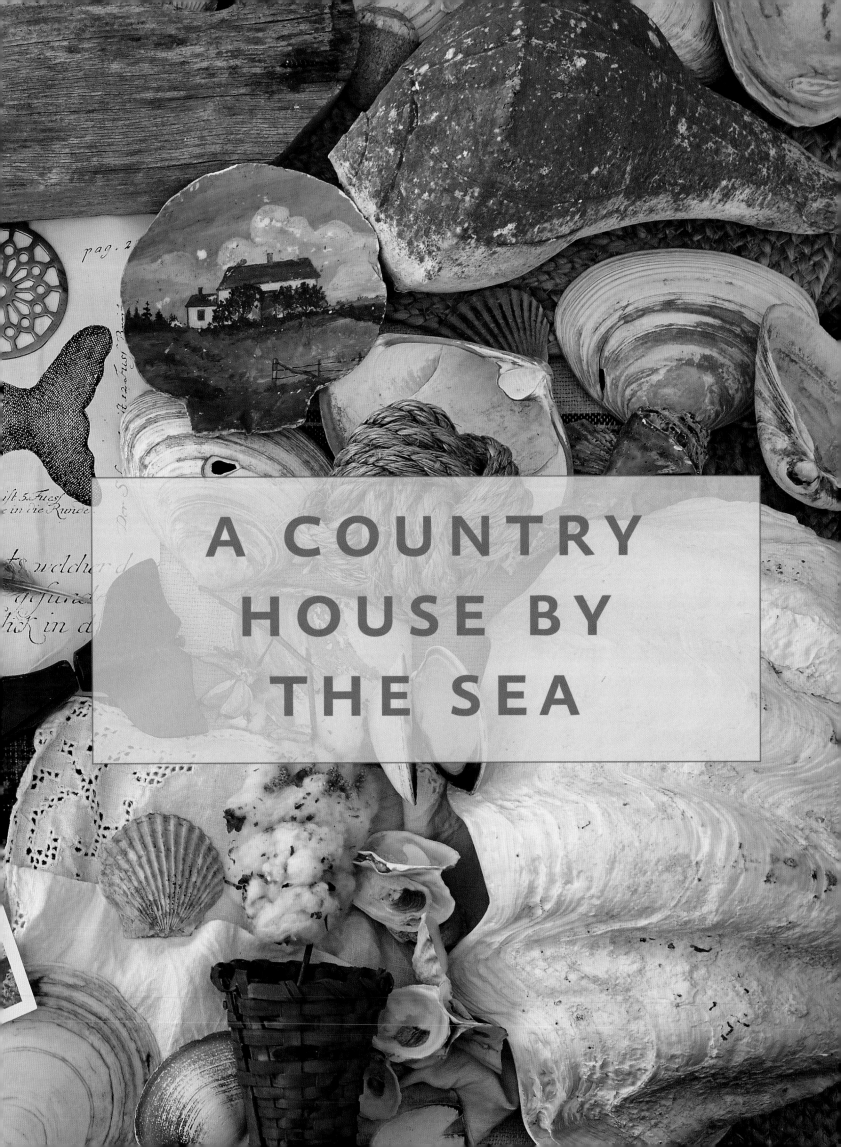

A COUNTRY HOUSE BY THE SEA

I adore Dana's style. Her historic home is wonderfully authentic, but it has every modern amenity. And it's so well thought out that there's no clutter. Her collected pieces are works of art. Everything has a story, inside and out.

Dana and I worked together more than a decade ago, and almost from the start we've been as close as sisters. When we met, I didn't expect her to be drawn to the country house life. *Unlike* me, she's tremendously accomplished in the tech world; anyone who knows her professionally would think she's modern to the core. But at home, she has a simple life that feeds her soul. It's a well-crafted balance.

She cherishes anything steeped in history with a good story to tell. For most people, that might mean a piece of vintage earthenware or a table with an interesting past. For Dana? She keeps buying *houses* with stories. My dear friend has taken the country house lifestyle to an entirely different level!

This is Dana's third old house. In a way, it's a family thing. Her parents were avid antiquers and would pack young Dana and her four siblings into the car for days of treasure hunting. Dana was a bit less than enthused by these outings. "I was always attracted to the story, though, to the meaning behind a thing. So I guess I was meant to do

left **Living with history.** Dana's historic country house compound includes the Dudley Pike Tavern (right), ca. 1790, and the red carriage house and barn, ca. 1811. Their layout out on this peaceful property makes for great entertaining!

this: to be a caretaker, someone who looks after things for a while and tells their stories."

Welcome to Dudley Pike Tavern, the property about forty minutes from the ocean that Dana calls home. It consists of the original tavern (actually, a 1763 Cape that became a tavern and inn in 1831), a newer addition (if you consider a couple hundred years old new!), a carriage house, and a barn. It's simple and quite primitive, with a few carefully considered updates hidden in plain sight. It's true to its roots and full of memories, some hundreds of years old—and Dana adds more every day.

"I think people live in houses but don't use them. There are people here *all the time*. This house has energy. It's not a museum! When I'm here, everyone knows that the bar is open. When I'm away, my friends come to stay. This place is an experience and it's always shared—that's important to me." Her warm, generous spirit certainly makes Dana's country house by the sea a place where everyone's always welcome.

"To me, country house style means approachable, livable, authentic. It means storytelling, and also, for me, caretaking. It's living simply and in a rich way based on where you are—rich as in content and texture. It has nothing to do with money. There are so many layers in a country house—it's all about how you choose to bring that to life." —Dana

right **Establish a theme.** Most of the nautical antiques and collectibles in Dana's cozy, understated Whale Room came from jaunts along the Maine coastline.

above, clockwise from top left **Accents in the garden.** An old punched-tin lantern guides guests to the tavern's door; dried gourds look like sculptures and shelter a few lucky little birds; a local craftsman built Dana's split-rail fence in a style that's true to the age of her home; Dana lines her walkways with oyster shells, each one a happy memory of a fine meal. "You're never having a bad day when you're eating an oyster," Dana says with a laugh.

opposite **Extend an invitation.** Sea stars twinkling in the transom and a hundred-year-old swan decoy beckon from the original entrance of the Dudley Pike Tavern.

above **Make every entrance count.** A new door leads to the mudroom. Its nine windowpanes flood the space with light, but it's still in keeping with the look of the house.

opposite **Add tonal texture.** In the spirit of country house style, what's useful is beautiful too. Straw bags are décor just waiting to be put to work.

above, clockwise from top left **Patina as a theme.** It took Dana more than a decade of hunting to amass her collection of unusually shaped cutting boards with wonderful wear; open shelves crafted of old wood display some of her rustic redware; a wood drain board from the 1700s is functional and graphic against the soapstone; touches of black are always welcome.

opposite **Design with function in mind.** A local woodworker built the shelving from a historical drawing that Dana carried with her for years. The washer and dryer are cleverly concealed behind the pantry doors.

above **Create an impromptu bar.** Champagne on ice in an old copper bucket and vintage Champagne glasses turn a weathered dry sink into a perfectly sophisticated bar.

preceding pages **Connect with the past.** Dana gutted a poorly updated kitchen to create a hardworking space in keeping with one that might have been there a hundred years ago. The cabinets are prefab, but she customized them with wooden knobs and pewter paint. The island's capacious work surface is an old tabletop from the previous owner.

opposite **Concealed conveniences.** Modern amenities are hidden behind a wall built and painted to look very old.

opposite **Update by editing.** In the 1800s, this was the main room of a busy tavern. Now, simply outfitted with just a few handcrafted pieces, it's a fresh, bright dining room.

above, clockwise from top left **Find the art around you.** A pair of antique bee skeps performs a country house hat trick: natural, modern, and sculptural; a rare nautical oil-on-board painting adds a graphic element; antique tin horns become modern art against the red 1820 stepback cupboard Dana found in Vermont; oil paintings, all about a hundred years old, capture the beauty of the Maine seacoast.

opposite **Mix in painted pieces.** An early nineteenth-century cupboard painted a washed ocean blue provides contrast—softly!—in the Whale Room, and complements Dana's collection of vintage crockery.

above **Show off your souvenirs.** An antique Norwegian bandbox that Dana picked up in Oslo looks like it was made to rest atop her eighteenth-century grain-painted blanket chest from Maine.

above **Offer a comfy seat.** Morning sunlight floods the Whale Room, warming the slipcovered Mitchell Gold rolled-arm sofa that Dana bought for her very first apartment. Guests gravitate to this well-worn-in, cozy spot.

opposite **Make room for a fabulous find.** Dana wasn't looking for it, but there it was: a gorgeous, rosy, eighteenth-century corner cupboard that she instantly pictured holding her favorite old corals and seashells.

above **Preserving history.** The original Dudley Pike Tavern sign welcomed guests from near and far until it went into storage in 1851. Years later, a local resident purchased it at auction, with the proviso that it would always remain in the town. Dana persuaded the then-owner to let her reunite the sign with the tavern, promising that the two will never be separated again.

opposite **A fresh take.** White walls and pewter-colored trim meet an edited arrangement of primitive furniture and accents with surprisingly modern results.

opposite **Create a charming retreat.** Whitewashed plaster walls make the guest room, one of two tiny upstairs bedrooms dating back to the tavern's stagecoach days, cheerful and inviting.

above **Wild and free.** A pitcher filled with Queen Anne's lace, abundant along any New England roadside, is a simple, charming touch.

above **Live inside out.** Dana's style—historical, relaxed, and serene—extends to her "outdoor rooms" too. From spring to fall, she and her friends pull weathered old Adirondack chairs up to the simple stone fire pit and enjoy the stars.

overleaf **Secret garden.** The thick branches of a 200-year-old apple tree reach wide to embrace and shelter a delightful spot for an intimate gathering.

opposite **Everything has a story.** The fragrant lilacs that surround the property date from the late 1700s, when Governor John Wentworth brought seedlings back from England to plant along the road to his summer home.

A COUNTRY HOUSE IN THE CITY

my and I got to know each other on Facebook. We hadn't met in person, but we "liked" each other a lot! I'd seen her blog, Maison Décor, and I appreciate and admire her French country style—it's cohesive, composed, and so *very pretty*, yet it's all approachable, accessible, and livable. It's also an amazing feat of imagination, as her home has undergone quite a transformation

Amy's house is in a city. It's a prefab, not even fifteen years old, on a 5,000-square-foot lot. The city's public transit serves her neighborhood. You can see the skyline from her door. It's not where or what you'd expect a country house to be. If there were ever a doubt that country house style is a state of mind, Amy's place provides proof that it's true!

Amy knew from an early age that different spaces made her feel different ways. Her father's job as an environmental engineer took their large family to places like Brazil, Pakistan, and Thailand; wherever they were, they rented a home and lived like locals. The moving around had its perks: "We got to visit the great cities of Europe, and I saw things that are a lot like things I live with today. I liked fancy. I liked gilded. I still do! My parents would joke, 'This kid has Champagne tastes!' I didn't know what it was called, I just knew that I liked Old World ambience—things that

left **Something from nothing**. Amy imagined a European country courtyard on her postage-stamp-size city lot and figured out how to make it happen.

seemed like they'd been around a while, that seemed like they might have a story."

When they moved back to the States for good, her parents found an old English Tudor in need of some repair. "Because I watched them and learned, I've always been attracted to older homes that need fixing up. There's so much satisfaction in that."

To say that she found her circa 2005 prefab a challenge would be an understatement. "I kept thinking, when do we move? I was playing a waiting game until I realized that I wasn't making my home my home. The thing I like about older houses is that they change over time; what starts as a square box gradually becomes something more interesting. I didn't feel comfortable here until I tried to age it, to give it that character." After adding some French doors here, aging a new wall there, the elements started coming together.

The sheer romance of her style also belies the fact that it's a lively, active home, where she and her husband raised four boys, so none of the prettiness has come at the expense of livability. It's the magic of Amy's country house in the city, where comfort is always in style.

"Country house style is relaxed and relates to nature. You're using the outdoors, it's part of how you live. Even if you're in a little Boston apartment, you have to have that kitchen window garden— there has to be that touch of nature. What we did with our small city lot proves that you can have a country house anywhere." —Amy

right **Looks soft, works hard.** *Pretty* is a hallmark of Amy's country house style, but so is *practical*. The comfy sofa has washable slipcovers and the sisal carpet is durable—essentials for a family with kids and a pup.

above, clockwise from top left **Elegant garden details.** A copper weathervane atop the garden shed in honor of Piper, Amy's English golden retriever; like my iron tuteurs, a vintage wire peacock bench becomes garden sculpture; Blushing Knock Out® roses are low-maintenance repeat bloomers all summer long; geraniums in a wire basket soften the approach to the front door.

opposite **A charming solution.** Amy and her son turned an old wooden crate into a multifamily birdhouse that also cleverly conceals an unsightly fireplace vent.

opposite **Adding personality plus.** The urn pediment, trim, and carriage lanterns read New England, loud and clear; they also impart a sense of history to a prefab home that's less than twenty years old. The granite-block steps leading to the inviting entrance porch are a visual reference to the courtyard.

above **A designated place for things.** In the entrance hall, the mirror set in an old window frame, the brass bunny, the basket, the lantern, and the botanicals combine to create a subtle garden vibe, bringing the outdoors in.

above **Pretty up a focal wall.** The living room's Woodlawn Blue walls seem like an extension of the sky in the landscape that Amy painted "as a lark." In another instance of character-generating country house ingenuity, she added appliqués resembling decorative plasterwork to a plain new fireplace surround to give it the French look she loves; she also used chalk paint to dye the antique sconce shades.

opposite **Buy it when you see it.** The star of the living room is a blue opaline French chandelier, ca. 1910. It's one of Amy's most prized antiques.

above, clockwise from top left **Isn't it romantic?** Vintage draperies take on new life as a pillow (an Amy original); purple glass flowers sparkle on an antique sconce; a single David Austin English rose from the garden perfumes the room; a baby grand piano, reflected in an antique Swedish mirror, isn't just for show—Amy's son plays.

opposite **Scale matters.** Compact and tall, a bonnet-top secretary fits perfectly between the front door and a living room window, enhancing the space while showing off a sweet collection of pink-and-gold lusterware.

opposite **Creative troubleshooting.** The problem: a door where there shouldn't be one. The solution: art! Happy with the results of her living room landscape, Amy painted this large canvas to conceal an unwanted door in the family room.

above **Add a graceful sculptural element.** An antique Mora clock, named for the Swedish town where they were first made, stands sentinel inside the front entrance.

opposite **Creating character.** To to add character to reproduction French Provincial–style dining chairs from the 1960s, Amy painted, stained, and gilded them. She and her son painted the table to simulate a well-worn, well-loved finish. The look is elegant, relaxed, fresh, modern, and definitely unfussy, in true country house style.

overleaf **Collecting over time.** Of her purple-and-white transferware, Amy says, "It's not very common, but I started finding it, and it started finding me. It's my main collection—and our everyday dishes. I don't believe in saving your 'best.'" Using your "best" every day makes every day special!

above **Pretty place settings.** Amy's elegant mix-and-match style never takes itself too seriously. In true country house fashion, attention to the little things creates big-scale beauty.

opposite **Petite and on point.** Today, Amy's small kitchen feels like *une cuisine* in a charming French cottage thanks to a few simple changes: the vintage tole chandelier; the elaborately detailed base of the island; the open shelves above the stove; and the pretty gingham check curtains.

above **Open shelving rules!** Despite their different looks, all six homes in this book share certain design elements. Open kitchen shelving is one of them.

opposite **Start with one special piece.** The tea table beside Amy's bed inspired a recent bedroom refresh. She took cues from its colors, texture, and details to reimagine this cozy space in her signature casual-luxe style.

above, clockwise from left **Putting together a pretty bedroom.** In the 1700s, an artisan in France or Italy took brush in hand and painted the table that Amy calls her favorite antique (quite a claim coming from a former antiques dealer); the pillow's pleated tabs form a stylized flower; the crystal chandelier with gilded leaves counterbalances the sisal rug and country baskets.

opposite **Dreaming up a little slice of paradise.** The compact, comfortable courtyard that Amy and her husband built using granite blocks, pea gravel, hardy plantings, and a lot of elbow grease has practical all-weather wicker furniture. Their kitchen garden and a shed are just steps away, up the hill to the left.

above **There's no place like maison.** The Maison Décor sign hung above Amy's first store; it seemed a natural fit here. As to the antique French day bed as outdoor accent—*magnifique*!

opposite **A recipe for charm.** Take one ramshackle old lean-to; employ one excavator; add a granite-block foundation; reinforce with cedar shakes; and install a French door from Craigslist. Enjoy a "new" garden shed for years to come! The old wheelbarrow belonged to Amy's husband's Swedish grandfather; they appreciate its connection to family history.

above **Make it personal.** Amy's decision to set a piece of cracked transferware into the shed floor was impulsive, whimsical, and so very her!

Nine & Sixteen
HOME
MARIEMONT INTERIORS

EST. 2010

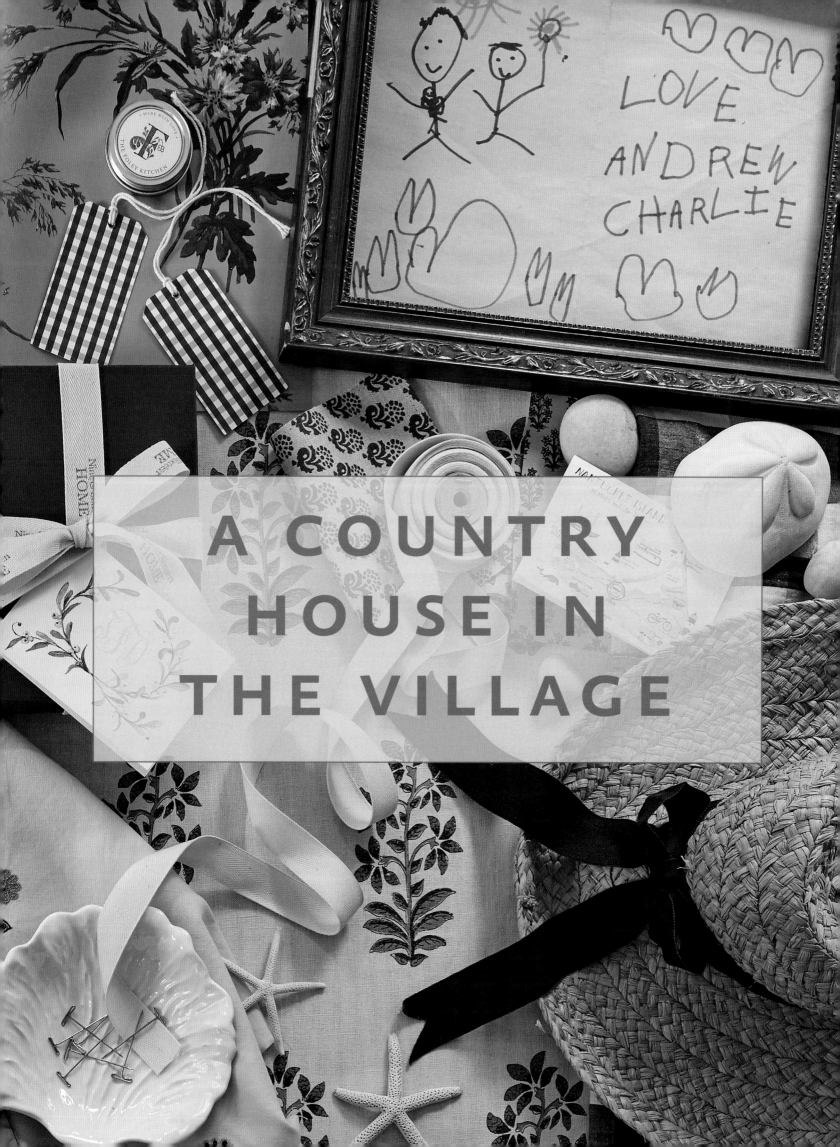

LOVE,
ANDREW
CHARLIE

A COUNTRY HOUSE IN THE VILLAGE

I'm a big fan of Tessa's blog, nineandsixteen, and she of mine. We're both interior designers and have a similar approach (though our results are quite different). We both feel that great interior design isn't just about decorative solutions but also involves creating a sense of warmth and welcome, and knowing that doing something with great thought and care is all it takes to make the ordinary extraordinary.

It's no surprise that her charming home is a perfect example of her design aesthetic. It reminds me of an English country cottage, even though it's a suburban 1950s Colonial situated in close proximity to its neighbors. A massive old oak shades the front yard, and cheerful blooms spill over the edges of window boxes, hinting at the happy vibe inside. It's tasteful, warm, welcoming, and ever so classic, just like she is.

In a way, the key to Tessa's design aesthetic—her deeply traditional center—led her to this place, a community where children walk to school, and ball fields, the village green, an ice cream parlor, and a movie theater are just down the street. If Norman Rockwell were a city planner, the result would be the delightful village in which Tessa lives.

Folks come here to put down roots and raise their families. The charm and tradition were irresistible to Tessa and her husband, Jim. "We knew we wanted to live there," Tessa recalls. "It's Mayberry-esque. It reminds me a little of New England, which is something we both love about it." Tessa

left **Honoring nostalgia.** Tessa's charming country house was built in 1950 as part of a planned community that was designated a National Historic Landmark in 2007.

and Jim lived in Boston for several years; New England—the coast in particular—holds a special place in their hearts and remains an influence on her style.

If there's anything closer to her heart than her family (and tradition, and her home), it's textiles.

"I have a bit of an obsession," Tessa confesses with a laugh. Many childhood summers were spent visiting her parents' relatives in Europe. The travel, though, isn't what captured her heart: "I can still picture in such detail the fabrics my aunt and my grandma used in their homes." Her appreciation and respect for these fabrics are innate, and her use of them is divine.

For Tessa, the collection is never the only point. "It's just as much about the experience of how I found something." Her treasures are touchstones of memories—I can relate! I also admire the way she uses her space. Nothing is precious or untouchable. There's no sense of a museum here, just a wonderful mix of past and present, attainable and real. Tessa has a deep connection to the traditional and a modern eye for what's fun and fresh. Her country house in the village truly honors tradition by changing it up.

"Country house style is, to me, a sense of a home that's timeless, warm, and welcoming. It goes beyond trends. It's loved and well lived in. It's not filled with tchotchkes, knickknacks, but with things that have meaning—the opposite of one-stop shopping. Nothing is ever finished in a country house; it's collected, layered." —Tessa

right **Add an artisan's touch.** The antique maple harvest table, scalloped slipcovers, silhouettes of Tessa's boys, and hutch are all handmade—the personal touch is a common thread in country house style.

above **Look for the authentic.** Patina shows the passage of time and accentuates pretty vintage details. With her first look at the old brass front door knocker (original to the house), Tessa knew—even before stepping inside—that this would be her home.

opposite **Marry a pretty pair.** An antique bamboo coat caddy and a new umbrella basket show off two of Tessa's collections, offer storage, and create the idea of a foyer where there isn't one.

above **Attract attention.** Blue-and-white transferware elevates an assortment of beachcombing treasures from family getaways to Cape Cod and Nantucket.

overleaf **Work with what you've got.** Country house style is beautifully flexible. Why replace everything as your own style evolves when you can adapt and reimagine instead? Tessa constantly finds new ways to keep her classics fresh.

opposite **Layer patterns.** Layered combinations of block-print patterns and classic English florals make Tessa's rooms feel cozy, special, and timeless.

COLONIAL STYLE

THE GREAT AMERICAN HOUSE Gil Schafer III

CHRIS MADDE

COLONIAL STYLE · CROCHET

THE GREAT AMERICAN HOUSE   GIL SCHA

CHRIS MADDEN THE SOUL OF A HOUSE

opposite **Choose soft and tactile fabrics.** Wherever you place it, older furniture creates instant collected-over-time appeal. In Tessa's sunny family room, slipcovers were all she needed to perk up those vintage pieces. Using primarily neutral colors for the seating lets an assortment of patterned pillows change up the look easily.

above **Consider dressmaker details.** Tessa is all about feminine details; she often adds pleats, ruffles, and bows to impart "her style" to furnishings.

opposite **Skirt a table.** Steps away from the front door, an oval table softens the lines of the sofa. Tessa covered it with a tailored, natural linen cloth that hangs to the floor. "It's the perfect spot to play around with different vignettes," she says.

above **Style a minibar.** An old wicker tray stocked with barware and spirits for seasonal cocktails rests atop a petite antique drop-leaf table—practical, inviting, and pretty!

above **Display everyday items.** Kitchen utensils that Tessa wants within easy reach are housed in various vintage ironstone vessels. Grouping the ironstone (or any collection) together ups the visual impact.

preceding pages **Add a farmhouse sink.** To achieve the English country kitchen look that Tessa has always loved, she opted for a farmhouse sink, new quartz counters, open shelving, and a light, airy paint color.

opposite **Be inspired.** The bright white sink pops against the muted colors of the gingham skirt and painted cabinets for a look that's modern and fresh.

opposite **Keep it focused.** Ready for a designer tip? The key to mixing patterns well is to use a focused palette. For Tessa, that's clearly blue and white!

above, clockwise from top left **Create a workspace that's personal.** Surround yourself with things you love: an embroidered fabric sample from Chelsea Textiles; a single fresh bloom is a pampering pick-me-up; an English scrubbed-pine table, antique Chinese porcelain lamp with a charming fabric shade, and Tessa's favorite floral chintz on the window help her get to work.

preceding pages **Start with a wallpaper.** In the master bedroom, a charming Thibaut wallpaper sets a cozy, cottage vibe. Natural linen on the gracefully curved headboard, ruffled bed skirt, and monogrammed pillows keep the whole space feeling smart and unfussy.

A COUNTRY HOUSE IN THE WOODS

M y dear friend Shawn and I met a few years ago through our respective jobs, and even if we hadn't, I am sure we would have found each other eventually, thanks to his delightful blog, thefarmhouseproject. In it he shares the trials and triumphs that "two city boys" (he and his husband, Kris) have experienced while renovating the oldest home in town—all with a lot of vision and humor, and on a strict budget. That's the stuff country houses are made of!

In 2012 or so, Shawn and Kris were itching to own a place of their own. The city was cost prohibitive and not exactly what they had in mind. "We'd watch HGTV and fantasize about fixing up a house in the country together," Shawn recalls. "I'm very hands-on, and there's nothing more rewarding than seeing the finished product turn out the way you'd hoped." Through friends, they honed in on an area where cows outnumber the human residents handily. After a Sunday drive, a visit to the farmer's market, and a stop at the antiques store, they were pretty sure they'd found their place.

Then it was just a matter of finding the house. "Kris wanted a tiny cottage in the middle of nowhere. I wanted a boarding house," says Shawn with a laugh. In discovering this five-bedroom historic beauty in the middle of nowhere, they both kind of got what they wanted!

left **The farmhouse project.** In 1800 the Woodman family, who owned the only wood and grain mills in the area, built this home, and a village grew up around it.

"We loved the architecture. It's a very historic farm-house with nods to different periods. It has the lines of a Dutch Colonial, Federal columns, and Victorian woodwork on the barn. We think that because the original owners were woodworkers, they had a good understanding of different styles, and they chose a variety because they loved them—and it all works.

"The first few weeks here, it was like camping out. We had air mattresses and wine, and a lot of time to decide what we wanted to do and what we could afford to do. In our loft in the city, we love midcentury modern industrial. We knew we couldn't bring that style into the new house, so we had to figure out how to decorate it without drawing on that aesthetic." To my eyes, the history of the home, the influence of the area, and their own personal passions blended into a perfectly balanced solution.

When these self-proclaimed city boys are in the country, they take full advantage of the space they have. Their favorite "room" is the deep, wide, wraparound porch, the repair of which was their first big project. "It's where we spend most nights, three seasons of the year," Shawn explains. "Looking out to the porte cochere, where a horse and buggy would have pulled up with visitors, it's like stepping back in time." There's no question that home extends well beyond the walls of Shawn and Kris's country house in the woods.

"To us, living a country house life means something apart from the hustle and bustle of the city. It's growing food. Doing projects ourselves. Shopping locally at the farmer's market or the antiques store. It's an authentic life at a slower pace." —Shawn

right **Just add flowers.** The handcrafted screen doors are original to the house. All they needed were new screens and a fresh coat of paint. Like me, Shawn and Kris say hello with flowers!

above **Natural wonder.** After seeing a Victorian still-life cloche in a local antiques shop, Shawn became "obsessed" with using found objects to create his own still lifes. Branches, moss, and countless other natural things found on their property give him plenty of material to work with.

opposite **Respect the architecture.** Shawn cleaned but didn't paint the interior side of the screen doors, giving the entrance an elegant, cohesive look.

opposite **Decorate with sound.** A retro record player looks right at home between two high-impact natural elements. The turntable and the records Shawn and Kris play on it are thrift shop finds. The hunt is part of the fun, and they never pay more than a few dollars for an album.

preceding pages **Defining an open space.** The great room, with its original American chestnut millwork and trim, is unusually large and open for such an old house. Shawn and Kris created the table out of a sewing machine base and an old tabletop they found at a yard sale. Occupying the center of the room, it defines the space around it.

above **Upcycled seating.** Another thrift shop score! An old sofa with beautiful lines needed only a reupholstering to become fresh and farmhouse ready.

above **Ready. Set. Done!**
Shawn snatched up the
dining chairs at a flea
market, painted them
white, and recovered the
seats, creating an elegant,
casual, and fresh look.

opposite **A not-so-common bar.** Behind the buffet-turned-bar, which holds the bottles of spirits that the
boys use to concoct the complex, creative cocktails they love, is a working pass-through to the kitchen,
where another built-in houses their collection of vintage cocktail and wine glasses.

opposite **A rejuvenated country kitchen.** When Shawn and Kris bought the house, the kitchen needed some love. To save money, they did almost all the work themselves. Their choice of white-on-white is both traditional and modern, true to a country house kitchen, and the copper farmhouse sink ties the wood and brick tones together. Shawn designed the island, which a local woodworker built of reclaimed wood.

preceding pages **Cook up something special.** The kitchen is warm and welcoming, practical, beautiful, and bright. Being there makes one want to grab a cutting board and get to work!

above **Hunting & gathering.** Original built-in cabinets (painted white by a previous owner) hold plates and old ironstone pieces that Shawn and Kris collect locally.

opposite **Make a statement.** Hung as art, a simple—and very big!—antique pitchfork feels sculptural and modern.

above, clockwise from top left **Artful arrangements.** Floating shelves made from reclaimed wood hold Kris's cookbooks and a collection of cake stands; a series of vintage kitchen utensils painted by a friend has a crisp look in modern black frames; a well-used butcher block from a general store holds ironstone and whatever's in season.

above **Create an art wall.** Silhouettes are rare and can be expensive, so it took Kris and Shawn several years to build their collection, which spans the eighteenth to the twentieth centuries. More recently, they found an artist in Pennsylvania who re-creates them; some of her works hang in the gallery, too, expanding the collection without costing a small fortune.

opposite **Then and now.** The Woodman family's exquisite woodwork was never "updated" with paint or a to-the-studs remodel. Thank goodness! Every turning is a testament to their good taste and skill.

above **Tailored and textured.** Let's talk about the deer in the middle of the room. The boys appreciate vintage taxidermy as a focal point and for the lodgy, woodsy tone it communicates so well. Flannels, plaids, and other menswear patterns give their bedroom a warm, comfortable, masculine feel.

opposite **See the potential.** Kris found this gloriously weathered chest at a yard sale for $15. The mirror, with its original glass intact, is attached.

opposite **Blending styles.** How do they do it? Another of the boys' incredible finds was this Victorian settee, which they acquired for $50 at a local auction and reupholstered in navy velvet. Its handsome curves set off and balance the room's masculine tone.

above **Bargain collecting.** You can find vintage brown bottles like these at just about any flea market, picker's clearinghouse, or antiques store, and they won't break the bank.

opposite **Embrace patterns on patterns.** Black-and-white toile de Jouy wallpaper prompted the feminine, botanical theme of the guest room. Everything about the room exudes charm, but the arrangement of mix-and-match green-and-white transferware above the bed is especially inspired!

above **Find the right balance.** A black mirror that Shawn designed in his days as a product designer for Ethan Allen complements the black-painted bed, tempers the honey tones of the dresser and floor, and makes the hardware pop.

opposite **Old-fashioned charm.** Since the house was built, there's been a picket fence around it. "We don't know if it's original, but it's very old," Shawn says of the sturdy, well-weathered fence in place today.

overleaf **Creating a relaxed alfresco space.** Shawn and Kris love few things more than entertaining, and they're incredibly warm, gracious hosts. Their hospitality doesn't start and stop at their door. It tumbles out onto the wide, wonderful porch than can hold dozens of guests with ease.

above **Surrounding serenity.** The barn beyond the cozy fire pit is original to the property. It once housed the family's horses and buggy; now it's Shawn's studio.

ACKNOWLEDGMENTS

Thank you to my mom, Charlotte, who introduced me to my very first country house, and to my late dad, John, who taught me to work hard and always listen to my heart.

To my husband, my love, my teammate, Murph: You are my rock. However crazy the ride, you've been there through every curve and bump in the road. None of this would have been possible without you.

To my sweet son, Conor, whose camera captures some of my favorite little moments: Your big heart, gentle nature, and warm spirit make this country house a wonderful place to call home.

To my dear friend Carol Hubner, who worked tirelessly on this book with great dedication, and who makes my vision a reality every day: I'm so happy you're all in!

To my dear friend and writer extraordinaire, Deb Golden: You get me. You capture my spirit and voice so eloquently. It's a labor of love and a joy to work with you.

To my lead photographer, DuAnne Simon, who never fails to amaze me with her breathtaking art and her perseverance: Working with you is pure pleasure.

To Darryl Arbesman, whose pictures capture the beauty and spirit of country house living effortlessly, and whose good humor can light up any day.

To Aida Kiernan, whose boundless energy and can-do spirit we are, happily, never without!

To Wendy, Dana, Amy, Tessa, and Shawn and Kris: Thank you from the bottom of my heart for your extraordinary generosity and hospitality, and for trusting us to share your country house style with the world. I hope we've made you proud.

To the exceptional legal eagle Roxanne Khazarian and PR star Caroline Galloway, who believed in me before I did: I am forever grateful for your friendship and encouragement, and for introducing me to Dana Newman, my "perfect fit" literary agent, who, with poise and savvy, took the idea for this book exactly where it needed to go.

To my publisher, Mark Magowan, his wife, Nina, and my editor, Jackie Decter, thank you for seeing something special in NMCH. Your books are works of art, and I am honored that my first book is part of the Vendome Press library.

To Anna Christian, for designing this book with sensitivity and making it true to who I am.

To my NMCH readers, friends, fans, followers, and community: Thank you for your encouragement and for inspiring me to write this book! Your loyalty means more than you'll ever know.

To my NMCH team, you know who you are: Your talent and unwavering support has created a rock-solid foundation for everything we're building together. I am so very excited for what the future will bring.

The seed of the idea that became Nora Murphy Country House took root through serendipity. Everyone I've met along the way has nurtured it. Letting it grow has been an act of faith, not just for me, but for the dear people in my life who have put their faith in me. Thank you, and I love you.

Nora Murphy's Country House Style: Making Your Home a Country House
First published in 2018 by The Vendome Press
Vendome is a registered trademark of The Vendome Press, LLC

NEW YORK
Suite 2043
244 Fifth Avenue
New York, NY 10001
www.vendomepress.com

LONDON
63 Edith Grove
London,
UK, SW10 0LB
www.vendomepress.co.uk

Distributed in North America by Abrams Books
Distributed in the United Kingdom, and the rest of the world, by Thames & Hudson

ISBN 978-0-86565-354-2

Publishers: Beatrice Vincenzini, Mark Magowan, and Francesco Venturi
Editor: Jacqueline Decter
Production Director: Jim Spivey
Production Color Manager: Dana Cole
Designer: Anna Christian

Library of Congress Cataloging-in-Publication Data available upon request.

Printed and bound in China by 1010 Printing International Ltd.
Fifth printing

All photographs by DuAnne Simon, with the exception of the following:
Darryl Arbesman: pp. 9, 10, 13, 28–29, 30–31; Conor Murphy: pp. 54–55; Nora Murphy: pp. 4–5, 17, 57, 59

page 2 A reproduction eighteenth-century shelf painted black gives the beautiful forms and textures of my collected corals the stage they deserve and makes a bold, graphic, sculptural statement.
page 3 The strength of this petite pieced heart is in its history: Provincetown artist Janice Walk created it using wood from an old snow fence on Race Point Beach and an 1880s lathe from Provincetown Town Hall.
page 206 I'm grateful for the beauty that blooms every day at my Connecticut country house—and for every one of you.